How to Make Someone Really Hate You ©

Based on the Psychology of Anger, Disappointment, Spleen and Peevishness

Oliver Jarvis

Contents

Testimonials

'This book, like, blew my mind. Now everyone hates me…it's been the greatest few months of my life'. Cedric the Familiar.

'It could be a joke disguised as a metaphor, or a metaphor disguised as a joke. What does that actually mean? It's not even a thing'. Olaf Pilosus

'This is simultaneously the scariest and funniest book I've read this year. It had me one minute rolling around in uncontrollable hilarity and the next in a state of bug-eyed psychosis'. Bethany the Third.

'Having read this book I can now safely say I hate Mr Jarvis. He's a damned idiot'. Anonymous English language teacher.

'This book is far creepier than those self-help ones about love. I think I need a shower to wash away the madness it has infested me with.' Ex-girlfriend.

'I think this book was written by an educationally sub-normal demon. WTF?' Anonymous South Sea Islander.

'I actually vomited onto my Kindle while reading this book. Then again, I had drunk 3 litres of White Lightning'. An Alkie.

About the Book

We should start on this journey together with a disclaimer. The hate dealt with in this book is in no way related to the bloody conflicts, religious disagreements, banking sectors or other political machinations that we humans seem fit to have become embroiled in.

It is rather a celebration of petty, everyday, street-level hatred. It's also a discussion of how to get your acquaintances, family (many of whom probably hate you already) and even your friends to loathe and despise you with every breath they can muster.

We will look at concrete and engaging examples throughout the book to outline clearly the steps required to make people not only dislike you, but actually hate you.

Hate is one of the strongest words in any language, and so a word of caution: whatever your motive for wanting a fellow human being to despise you, please take the content of this book with a pinch of salt. The methods described really do work, and if used to their fullest extent can cause minor mayhem, disruption to your private life and even public disorder.

Enough said, let's get started!

About the Author

Oliver Jarvis was an English language teacher for 18 years in various countries before finally becoming fed up to the back teeth with it in 2012.

He then started 'Global Proofreading and Copy-editing', a company which specialises in online English language correction. Most of the clients are at university in non-English speaking countries and need their dissertations, theses and essays checked and corrected. The business is expanding rapidly and the website receives 1000's of hits a week: www.globalproofreading.com Global Proofreading and Copy-editing is fast becoming one of the biggest companies of its kind in the world.

Sickening, don't you think? Yet another nauseating 'success story' which probably already has you feeling vaguely annoyed. Good! I could easily sit down and write books with well-worn titles such as 'How to start your own Business', or 'Make £1,000,000 in a year', which would already join the saturated market of 'How to...' or 'Self help' literature. And these books are always about how to do something positive or useful! How irritating.

So Oliver has founded a series called the 'Anti-self Help Heap'[©]. The books in this series are dead-set against the whole 'Self help' movement; they could be taken either a serious aid (in this case for making people hate you) or maybe a bit of a chuckle at times.
Oliver Jarvis, February 2014

Part 1: Step-by-Step

Of course every culture, every society, every person is different, but I would like to claim that feelings of anger, irritation, peevishness and even hate are universal. Even Buddhist monks have been involved in some fairly serious rioting over the years! In this section a series of real-life incidents are described, where mere spleen can evolve into genuine hatred by using the simplest of techniques.

The Man on the London Tube

Let's start with the proverbial 'man on the street' (or the London Tube in this case) and move step-by-step from acquaintances to colleagues to family, and finally to best friends.

So, it's 6pm on a Friday evening. A Tube train packed and rammed to the rafters has just pulled into Victoria Station. Unsurprisingly, a large proportion of the passengers need to alight in order to continue their journey onwards and upwards to Victoria Railway Station itself.

When the doors of the Tube train open after yet another inexplicable delay there is a robust surge in that direction. Tempers are frayed, people are tense and fractious. It's an unpleasant experience for everyone.

You need to get out of the train. Because of the sheer numbers of people behind you pushing forwards, you in turn inadvertently push the person in front of you. He's a short, blond young man, smartly turned out, wearing designer glasses, obviously a commuter. And obviously not acquainted with Newton's Third Law. He says 'watch what you're doing, we're all getting out here', or words to that effect. Rude.

Does this man hate you? He may appear to from his tone of voice and body language, but he is merely irritated like everyone else trying to exit this ghastly Tube. Now is your Golden Opportunity to foster that irritation into hatred. He thought it was the end of the matter, that you would be instantly lost in the colossal crowds, but not so! You stick right behind him all the way up the escalator upbraiding him loudly for being such an arse. You follow him into the station, continuing your tirade. By which time he is definitely worried and almost certainly now hates you for making a spectacle of him in such a public place.

Acquaintances

These are people you know, but who are not really your friends. You might acknowledge their presence when passing them in the street, you go for drinks with them as friends of friends, you try to avoid many of them at all costs.

Why would you want to avoid an acquaintance? Here's another case study: A very good friend (let's call him 'D') has been abroad for a year on a work contract and has just arrived back in your home town. You are keen to meet up for drinks, and arrangements are duly made to gather on the town common (it's summer and glorious weather). Unfortunately your recently returned pal has a lot of other 'good' friends who will also be present at the festivities. For you they are just acquaintances, and they don't hate you, so it's no big deal, right? At first everything is going fine, the beer is flowing, the music is pumping, there's even a smallish bungee jump attached to a crane as entertainment.

Unfortunately the party starts to wear a bit thin after a couple of hours as you haven't been able to speak to 'D' properly yet; one or two of your acquaintances are monopolising him. You feel jealousy and rage. You're also feeling somewhat pole-axed due to the effects of several pints of lager and the sun beating on your unwisely uncovered head.

Now you hate those monopolising bastards. How do you get them to hate you back? There are a few ways, but by far the most effective one, and is to vomit down the sleeve of one of their jackets (which should be laid out on the ground). You then drunkenly pass out so it's abundantly clear who the culprit is. This acquaintance will now hate your guts, especially if he puts the jacket on before realising what has happened! And this kind of incident has good mileage as it'll be remembered for years to come.

Colleagues!

Now colleagues are an absolute gold mine for hatred. A 'hate mine' if you will indulge the metaphor. Anything from funny looks, to leaving the photocopier jammed, to droning and moaning, to texting while pretending to engage in a conversation; these can all cause juicy levels of annoyance and resentment to fester beneath the wafer-thin veneer of politeness in the working environment. However fascinating all this might seem, there are far more dastardly deeds afoot between colleagues, some even involving grand larceny. And this next case study involves just that:

Ok, so you are a manager, you have a certain amount of clout, the pay grade to hire and fire. You are interviewing for an important role and there is one candidate who is ideal. She's hyper-friendly, hard-working, punctual, reliable, in fact the model employee. Do we dislike her yet? Of course not; she's too much fun, she's full of energy, she can engage you in challenging conversations. And she smokes, which is always a bonus.

Life moves on, you move away from Manchester to take up a 12-month contract in the oil fields of Algeria. But what to do with all your possessions? You've just bought a £2500 black leather sofa with footstool, a £300 lamp, plus kitchen utensils and appliances worth around £1000. Not to mention an array of electrical items.

There's no way this lot is going to the Sahara desert, aṣ-Ṣaḥrā' al-Kubrā. Not on your watch. Too dusty. Too sofa leather-cracking. Your vivacious new colleague comes up with a very generous solution…why not store all your items in her secure garage free of charge until your return from the Middle of Nowhere? Why not indeed? So a while later you hire a van and take all your worldly possessions to this lock-up, unload, head for the airport and get a triple J D down your neck pronto. Any hate lurking yet? None at all? Can we see what is going to happen to our unsuspecting hero??

You're not entirely brainless. You ask a friend to check up on your gear from time to time. It's all fine, snug and toasty in its tarpaulin and bubble wrap. Then. Then indeed. Around 6 months later another set of people (strangers to you from Oldham) also start to store some of their (rather rank) belongings in the same place. You all share the same set of keys. Alarm bells begin to ring…there's something not quite right.

And too right! One fine day, shortly after your return from the Land of Endless Dehydration you and your friend discover the lock to the garage has been changed. Heavy-duty, too, tricky to get past. Needless to say, your colleague has vanished, or vanished in the sense that she doesn't answer your calls, your emails or her damn front door. You don't hate her. You are rightly pissed off; you need your gear, man! Come on! Eventually you commit the crime of the century and break the lock to the accursed garage. It's empty. Totally empty, even immaculately swept. You've been had.

Now you hate her for obvious reasons. But I bet she hates you a lot more. The person you hate most in your life is always the one you have wronged, not vice versa.

Now chew on that for a minute my fine herd of Fresian cows, because we have the Grand-Daddy of them all coming up….

Family

Family is a very tricky one to deal with. The amount of pain, anguish and sorrow caused by hatred within families is unfathomable, a bottomless pit of emotional horror and abuse. We won't go there. There is plenty of other literature available on all aspects of this. Just go on Amazon and browse.

However, the mood of this book is supposedly light, in spite of the scary ease with which you can make people hate your very guts. So I'm going to relate a tale where one family member caused his very own father to hate him. For a few seconds at least.

Growing up as a boy can be crazy fun, an absolute blast most of the time, but us chaps do tend to get ourselves into unfortunate scrapes and accidents. In some families, under the rule of certain fathers, there is no room for cry-babies, pussies, sissies or wimps. Sports often play a large role in a child's life and by God you'd better be good at them.

So it's high summer and you are in the garden. You are seven years old, barefoot, apparently alone, enjoying kicking a football around the lawn. The ball comes to rest next to a low brick wall surrounding a flower bed. Feeling particularly enthused and energetic about the next kick, you boot the ball as hard as you can. You miss the ball and the big toe of your right foot cracks into the wall at top speed, shattering the bones within.

The pain is incomprehensible, grotesque and vast. You had no idea such levels of physical agony could exist! All you can do is lie on the ground, not crying, but making a kind of pitiful moaning sound. As you lie there rocking back and forth, utterly consumed by this terrible pain only a broken bone can produce, your father appears suddenly and shockingly; a baleful giant from your perspective on the ground. He is angry and tells you to get up and stop being such a sissy.

When you are unable to do this due to the fact that your toe is pulverised your father becomes incensed, and at that second you can see in his eyes he hates you, the snivelling wretch on the ground crying over nothing. In his defence he doesn't know your toe is broken, but still, it all seems very harsh, and he hates you. Task accomplished!

This is one of the billions of ways to get a family member to hate you; it's rather a strange method, I agree, but one which works nonetheless.

You get your revenge. Later that summer your father is wading in the sea in Cornwall, he accidentally kicks an underwater boulder and breaks the very same toe you did a few weeks before!

Best Friends

This one is also a real humdinger. History is littered with perfectly good friendships which have turned sour and died. Friends can become enemies at the drop of a hat. But what about your best friend of 20 years? It's going to take something extra special to earn his/her hatred.

Here is a potted version of a history of two great friends. You met him (known as 'P') at university in 1991 and hit it off straightaway. Common interests, a similar sense of humour, plenty of drugs and booze. You know what I'm talking about. After university you stay in touch, and even though most of the time one of you is abroad you stay in touch using snail mail, email, texting, and finally Skype.

In 2003 P buys a flat and settles in Croydon. You go to visit for a couple of weeks once year and the good friendship never fades. You have a real laugh together. Until in 2007 he meets the all-important Love of his Life (known as B). You don't like her and she doesn't like you, mostly because during your annual visits to P you get drunk and 'lead him astray'. You and B both feel jealousy and resentment. There's trouble brewing for sure, but B has to put up with it as your friendship with P is still going strong and is in its 17th year.

In 2009 you finish yet another 12-month contract abroad, this time in Argentina. You have a new girlfriend so you are looking to settle down in London. The only real problem is finding somewhere to live. You need to be physically in a place to do this effectively.

P comes up with a brilliant solution to this quandary. He and B are going to visit family for a month a week or so after you return from the Land of the Pampas. You can house-sit for a month while you find your own place! A perfect solution all round? Of course it isn't. Look...

You arrive, move in and try to be as inconspicuous as possible for the week that P and B are still in the house. P is fine, but B is making you feel more and more unwelcome. Comments muttered about storage space; your not being able to use the kitchen or dining table; the house is freezing and filthy; one time she even has a go at you for daring to use the tumble-drier and pulls your towels out of it still wet. Something is really badly wrong. She hates you and wants you gone, even though it's only a few days before they head off on their family visit. At this stage you don't know why this particularly virulent hatred has arisen, so I cannot offer advice on how to bring it about, other than simply existing and breathing in someone else's house!

One day, soon enough, the inevitable happens. P summons you to 'have a chat'. He and B want you gone as soon as possible. The reason being B 'wants her house back'. Apparently she never wanted you there in the first place (in spite of the fact that you were there at her invitation). So, unsurprisingly, you now hate her…they are giving you less than a week to find somewhere else to live. Anyone who has rented in London knows this is impossible within this small amount of time. This hatred is not difficult to explain…kick someone out of your house when they have nowhere to go and they will despise you for it.

So you are being thrown out onto the street by your supposed best friend of 18 years. This happens the next day…you leave. You don't hate your friend P, but the same truth goes for this as for the furniture thief:

The person you hate most in your life is always the one you have wronged, not the one who has wronged you.

And as for forgiveness? Forget about it! Harbour a grudge, keep that hate alive and boiling away; you never know when you might need it.

Part Two: This is as Good a Start as Any

The purpose of this book is not to analyse or define hatred, or even especially to work out its root causes. We are all human and understand the answers behind these issues all too well. This is a 'How to' book turned upside-down; an 'Anti-how to' book. So of course here we are concerned with the Devil's work itself, the all-important 'How'.

'Existension'

In order to continue we need to bring a new word into the English language. It's a stunning fact in itself that this word is not already in use anywhere; it never has been as far as we can be reasonably aware. The word is 'existension'.
It has two main meanings. I'll define them in a conversational way rather than giving a precise dictionary-style definition.

> **1.** You are walking along a pedestrionised High Street mid-morning somewhere in the UK. There is the mother of all street markets taking place; the longest in Europe if you believe the rumours, two rows of beautifully vibrant stalls selling fruit and veg, underwear, sweets and

biscuits, cheap clothing, all the usual produce. It's a weekday and it's busy. You generally like to walk fast, especially where shopping is concerned, but here, on this market-cluttered, pram-infested street you are continually being forced to walk at a slower-than-usual pace simply due to other people going about their business. You don't have to be anywhere at a certain time, no doctor's appointment, no signing on, no work. So you have no real reason to be annoyed at being slowed down by a busy market.

In fact you have a day off and are on the way to the supermarket. There is no reason for any negative feeling whatsoever. The crux of the matter is to do with your preferred walking pace and your resulting emotions towards your fellow human beings, who are slowing you down and preventing you from doing precisely as you please. They are dithering and procrastinating, blathering and loitering. You resent their existence. This feeling is known as 'existension'.

2. The second meaning of existension is very close to existential angst; the difference lies in the nuances of the emotions involved. The latter expression is a feeling of anxiety or nervousness about the very fact of your existence. You contemplate the cold, empty, pitiless universe and you feel sick with fear. Jean-Paul Sartre is the man to read for this kind of thing. His short novel 'Nausea' would be a good place to start.

So, existension: your five-year-old daughter leads a happy and healthy existence. She attends school, has friends, is reasonably bright, and is in good health. In other words, everything is as 'normal' as it could be in our 'Western' UK society (and many similar societies). Except for one thing, which because of her age is considered cute. In the morning, when you switch on the light her to wake her up, she shouts out 'Oh, no, not again'! She's not nervous or afraid, merely annoyed to find the world exactly the same as it has been every morning she's woken up in that place. This feeling of annoyance towards existence itself is existension. We are asking the question:
'Why do things have to be this way?' 'Why have we organised a society where we have to leave a perfectly warm and comfortable bed in the morning?'
I'm sure most of us experience existension regularly. Annoyance at existence itself.

Taking it to the Next Level

Fortunately the kind of hate we are dealing with in this book is quite rare. Everyday, petty concerns leave us irritated, stressed and peevish, but not filled with hatred and loathing.

Ninety-nine percent of our negative feelings towards our fellows remain at the existension level. So how do we make this huge raft of people really hate us? Why don't they despise us at first sight? Even celebrities who we usually find particularly annoying don't incite choking rage whenever we see them on television or online.

So is it even possible to make the man on the street hate us? Let's go back to that busy market. You feel annoyed by being held up and obstructed at every turn, so it must stand to reason that other people feel the same way. Some people like to walk quickly. Others like to saunter along in their own sweet time, pushing their ultra-wide push-chairs crammed with kids. Who would you like to hate you for a few minutes? It can't be everyone, so you have to choose.

The fast-walking type is more likely to be tense and highly-strung and so there is a good chance he will take the emotional leap from existension to hatred more easily. The market is a good place for this experiment, but I would suggest a major Tube Station in London at rush hour is more conducive to the emotion we are trying to trigger. Remember the case study we looked at earlier at Victoria Station?

Commuters have one aim in mind after work; to get home. Anything which disrupts this journey is going to piss them off. If they have to change Lines, this often involves lengthy walks along narrow corridors, climbing up and down stairs and riding escalators, often with the added torture of hearing a train pull into the platform they are trying to reach. They have to get that train! The Tube is notoriously fickle and commuters can be delayed for hours at the drop of a hat. Signal failure, body on the line, blizzards, all of these can kick off at any second so they have to get that train!

One Sure-fire Method

You've read the case studies. Now we are actually going to do it; here is one method which will make at least one person hate your guts, at least momentarily. Here we go:

Get yourself onto the Central Line on a hot summer's evening, once again at around 6pm. It's extremely busy, the temperature is around 35-40 degrees, people are crammed into trains like livestock, even the platforms are impossible to move along at anything even approaching a decent pace. The tense commuter type is easy to spot; smart clothing but casual shoes for the trek home, plus some kind of backpack, and even a book to ease the pain. He knows what he's doing and where he's going. And so do you.

So, Tottenham Court Road platform whizzes into view, the train stops, and several hundred people commence the fairly long and complex change onto the Northern Line. There are tourists, bless them, who don't know where they are going; there are families with small children; there are obese people, elderly people, people on crutches; there are people who are looking at their phones; there is even the occasional unfortunate person who has forgotten to take his medication and is labouring under some kind of terrifying psychosis. This is the section of humanity clogging up the platforms, corridors and stairways. They are helping your cause by increasing the atmosphere of tension! We'll refer to them as 'cloggers'. (This word already exists in the English language meaning 'one who makes clogs'.) Here, in the fetid rush hour Tube, the second new meaning I hope is abundantly clear.

Then there are the thousands of commuters all trying to dodge, weave, dance and hop around this mass of cloggers. Some brave souls even balance between the yellow line and the platform, a deadly tight rope centimetres from death by Tube Train. These ones are your targets! They are already stressed out, feeling the existension, so it's time for you to act.

There's always a bottle-neck where Tottenham Court Road platform narrows into the corridor leading the Northern Line. Choose your man; he's the one who has spotted a rare and fast-closing gap between two foreign language students and a middle-aged lady carrying what appears to be a cat in a basket. You deftly step into this gap, just sealing it at the last second. The commuter, who was striding along too fast for the situation, stumbles into your back. No problem? You make it one by turning round and telling him to watch where he's effing going.

Now we are entering the arena of confrontation. The commuter has not yet reacted, but you keep ahead of him, skilfully blocking any gap to impede his progress. He must surely be pissed off, but no hatred yet. Yet as you approach the stairs to the platforms you can hear the tantalising sound of a train approaching the Northbound platform. The commuter needs to be on that train if it's for High Barnet. Bad adrenalin kicks in. There might not be another one for 5 or 6 whole minutes!!!!

This is where you step up your game. Slow down, crouch to briefly fiddle with the hem of your trousers, stare at the ceiling whistling the theme music from Love Story. If the apoplectic commuter tries to pass you, stick out a foot to make him stumble. You mount the stairs, round the corner and there it is, the High Barnet train. The doors are still open! The commuter makes a dash for the nearest door; fortunately it's one of those single doors at the end of a carriage so there's only room for single-file entry. You are ahead of him and there's just time for both of you to make it onto the train. You can even see a few empty seats!

Just as you are putting your foot into the carriage you pause, mutter something about needing the Mill Hill train, pause again until the doors start closing and then retreat back onto the platform. The train pulls away and rattles out of view. Your commuter is incensed; you've blatantly been delaying and obstructing him. You've directly caused him to miss his train and he quite rightly now hates your guts. Congratulations!

The next train to High Barnet is in eight minutes.

Delving Deeper

It's all very well going through life making random strangers hate us; this is child's play, as we have seen in the two London Tube incidents related earlier.

We now need to delve much deeper and make people 'fall in hate' with us. There are many Self-help books explaining in minute and creepy detail how to make someone fall in love with us. Here we are dealing with the opposite emotion. How can we make someone dislike us at first meeting and then develop this antipathy into loathing? This is a big question indeed.

One of the most important points to bear in mind here is that if you want someone to fall in hate with you there needs to be some kind of ongoing relationship; a family member, a friend, a boyfriend or girlfriend, a teacher, a colleague, anyone we meet long-term in order to nurture that festering emotion.

It's not easy at all to hate someone for a long period of time. The case studies we have looked at so far all relate one-off incidents where the loathing is bound to wear off in time. So in order to succeed in making a specific person hate you in a profound and lasting way you have to be around them a lot. You cannot hate properly from a distance; you have to show that person you are a part of their life; a permanent disagreeable fixture.

Once you have shown that person they cannot get rid of you at all easily they will start to really despise you.

Why you?

The Night out on the Town

So why would a certain person start to feel hatred towards you rather than someone else? Imagine you are on an evening out on the town with a group of people; some are your friends, some are friends of friends, some are mere acquaintances, some may even be total strangers, yet part of your group. Here we have the ideal scenario! You should start by singling out one person to target for your hate experiment. Long after the evening is over you should stick in this person's mind as someone who is highly unpleasant and to be avoided at all costs. I'm not referring to obviously vulgar tactics such as insults or violence (although of course these tactics work in the short-term, you might be forgiven, which is certainly not something we are trying to achieve here).

Here are a few tactics you can use to put someone off you right from the start:

- Physical attributes. We are concerned here with physical attributes which you can control, not ones you are born with. I'm not suggesting you stop washing for a fortnight before your night out and walk around stinking like a rhesus macaque. This is too obvious. More subtle signals could include: a man missing a part of his face when shaving; not bothering to wash or brush your hair; taking no heed at all to your clothing, just sling on whatever comes to hand (I've found tight brown corduroy trousers and a pink shirt to be effective); making sure you have sweat stains under your armpits; not bursting whiteheads on your face – theirs nothing like a juicy growth of pus to put people off. Then there's garlic...eat some raw before going out. The effects of this alone are just horrible for anyone in the vicinity.

- Eye contact. When trying to attract someone you should hold their gaze for slightly longer than is usually socially acceptable. The key word here is 'slightly'. This is easy to remedy. Either don't meet their gaze at all or stare into their eyes to the point of making your unfortunate new 'friend' feel uncomfortable and look away. I would recommend a method used by Aleister Crowley. During conversation he would appear to be looking straight through you and focussing on a point a metre or so behind your head. This must be very disconcerting and is bound to start the inklings of negative emotions. You already appear weird!

- Weirdness is not enough though. This book is not called 'How to make Someone Think you are really Weird' (although there will be such a title as part of the Anti-Self Help Heap). Anyway, you are doing the Crowley thing with your gaze; staring straight through your victim in order to unnerve him. Always bear in mind you are on a fun night out; people expect you to be sociable, affable and extravert. They expect you to smile. Of course a genuine smile attracts people, so you must make yours as creepy and inappropriate as possible. Link the Crowley gaze and the smile together; this can produce a very repellent effect. Smile far too much, or not nearly enough. Never smile when your interlocutor says something amusing. Always smile when they mention some kind of misfortune or unfortunate incident. Now you appear creepy as well as weird. The person you are talking to now most probably dislikes you and will try to move on to talk to someone else in the group. This is when you really need to step up your game.

- Do not, under any circumstances, let your victim leave you yet. Hopefully social etiquette will force him to chat for a while longer. This is where your arrogance has to come to the fore. Talk about yourself, disparage others. Mention your various achievements. Generally the more impressive the achievement, the more annoying it is. Tell them you were single sculling champion twice in a row at university. Mention the fact that you were recently promoted to some highly-paid position. Don't forget to talk at length about your daily work-out routine and 5-mile run. Whenever your new-found friend attempts to say anything whatsoever about himself, dismiss him, interrupt him and use one of your Crowley stare-smiles. By now you have hopefully gone in his mind from being weird, to creepy, to being a self-obsessed wanker. You are making real progress! Hate is on its way.

- As the evening goes on your group changes venues; crowded pubs, bars, and eventually night-clubs. The dynamics will change as some people become drunker than others. You won't be able to remain with your victim for the entire evening as by now he will actively be trying to avoid you. Let's assume the worst-case scenario doesn't happen with him deciding to go home. No, he's sticking around. So you need to become loudly and obnoxiously drunk. Sit next to him whenever possible and yell directly into his ear with your garlic, alcoholic, stale cigarette breath. This will surely be more than he can tolerate. He may even tell you to back off. You don't and remain his faithful companion for the rest of the evening. Stay to the bitter end and join him on his journey home as far as possible, drunkenly telling him rambling, pointless and utterly tedious stories about your life in full earshot of everyone on your chosen public transport. We can now safely say he hates you, but in order to consolidate this you need to be part of his group whenever he goes out for a night on the town. The more he has to associate with you, the more he will hate you. And be assured, your disgusting behaviour will not go unnoticed by others. Objective achieved!

The Hated Director

As we saw earlier with the 'colleague furniture theft' incident, there are a number of unusual and even bizarre ways to earn the hatred of a much-liked colleague. In most places of work there is so much scope for becoming a figure of hate that an entire book could be written on just this subject. Here we are going to focus on a little-known industry in the UK: Teaching English as a Foreign Language (TEFL).

TEFL

Every year thousands and thousands of foreign language students come to the UK to study English. They attend hundreds of English language schools up and down the country from Aberdeen to Falmouth. Some stay for a week, some for years. They come from every country in the Globe. For example, relatively recently, I had a class of 8 students. They were from Oman, Venezuela, Saudi Arabia, Thailand, China and Brazil, and they got on famously. In fact, when you have a class like this and they are all chatting away it makes you wonder why human conflict arises in the first place. Anyway, I digress.

Back to the central figure in this seemingly hate-free zone. We are referring to the Director of Studies, also known as the DOS. If you are fortunate enough to secure this job then the possibilities for becoming a figure of hate are almost endless; you can earn the loathing of not only your management colleagues, but also the teachers, the admin staff and the students. In a large school this is potentially over 1000 people!

Sheer incompetence

Appearing to be incompetent at your job is the first step towards earning the hatred of your management colleagues. There will be weekly meetings; arrive late, yawn throughout, don't take notes, even drift off to sleep if you have the balls to do that in front of your boss.

As DOS you will in theory have a lot going on; multi-tasking is required for most of your working day, so minutes of the meeting will be sent round later that day with an action plan for each member of the management. Action is key! Print your copy of the minutes off, write an expletive at the top and then either screw it into a ball and toss it out of the window, or leave it in plain sight on your desk. Do not take any action! This means, for example, when the new term arrives there will be no new course books for any of the students! A total cock up! You may receive a verbal warning, about which you appear not to give a shit, but from then on you do the barest minimum to keep your job.

Your colleagues/boss are neither stupid nor blind; they can see what you are up to! But you are protected by UK Employment Law as long as you keep doing the absolute minimum to keep your job. After a while they will really start to dislike you, especially as they are the ones who will often have to rectify your imbecilic blunders and blatant laziness. And when an outside inspection comes around, they will hate you, simply because someone will have to do extra admin and preparation work that you have neglected. Another warning? Bothered? These warnings are soon wiped from your now impressive HR file.

The Teachers

Right, this is very important. TEFL teachers in the UK have a very raw deal. They are ludicrously underpaid, usually have no proper contract to speak of, and have to work long hours in often cramped and stifling conditions. Imagine a hot day in London; you are crammed into a tiny classroom with 20 students and no air-conditioning. You can't open a window because of a pneumatic drill working away right outside and the quality of the air is almost certainly carcinogenic. It's a 3-hour lesson with one 15-minute break. The conditions are already intolerable. The teachers, even the most sanguine and chilled-out, are feeling 'existension' to the max. Why should things have to be this way? Why?

You are their line manager, the person they come to with all their requests, complaints, melt-downs, resignations etc. The least they can expect for all their hard work and low pay is a smiling face and some reassurance that things will improve.

This is where you get to work to earn not only their disrespect but also their hatred in many cases. Appear to listen to their requests for this and that; a fan in Room 21, a TV that actually works somewhere in the damn school, fewer students per class, all perfectly reasonable, right? Right. But you do nothing. You sit at your desk yawning, perhaps picking at the skin on your thumb, you go for 'walks', you smoke endless fags, you even snort a line or two of cheeky coke in the bogs. You do anything except fix that fan, buy a new TV, and as for student numbers, forget about it! Nothing changes or is going to change, and this becomes apparent to your teaching team a few weeks into your new DOS job. As we've seen earlier, incompetence leads to lack of respect, then to active dislike and in a few more easy steps to that all-important hatred.

Unnecessary stress

Teachers of a foreign language understandably like to be left in peace to teach their classes. As DOS you must avoid that learning-conducive peace and quiet at all costs! Throw admin at your teachers by the bucket-load, most of it apparently a total waste of everyone's time: for example, weekly lesson plans to be put on the walls of every classroom; nobody, least of all the students, is ever going to read them as they are tacked to the notice board with one drawing pin (there's an perennial lack of pins in your school) between some students' pieces of writing about their visit to Windsor or some such UK hell-hole, and a Health and Safety notice (also ignored by all). Work-done books, the actual point of which remains vague, are checked daily by your increasingly irrational and arbitrary reign of terror.

And then there is the 'lateness rule'. No student is allowed into their lesson after a certain cut-off point, usually 10 or 15 minutes into the lesson. This is one rule you enforce to the point of madness. You march round all the classrooms, you physically restrain students form entering their lesson, or even throw students out who are now actively taking part in a useful piece of English language input. You glare and scowl at the students through the small window in each classroom door. You are making a mockery of the whole learning process.

This pisses off the teachers as it severely disrupts their thoughtfully planned lessons, it pisses off the students who will not get their all-important attendance for visa compliance, and it pisses off the admin staff, who have to sit and listen to a litany of excuses and complaints in barely comprehensible English. This is a good breeding ground for hate to build up between pretty much everyone and the DOS, who in actual fact doesn't really have to enforce this 'lateness' rule at all.

Holidays and Pay

Everyone knows there are two things you should never, ever mess with; the holidays and pay of your members of staff. As we've already seen, teachers of English as a foreign language in the UK are sorely treated, so the least they can expect is some time off as and when needed, and to be paid properly and on time.

So, here's a good case in point: a teacher needs 3 days off in a couple of months. She fills in a 'holiday request form' and brings it to you in your office during her break. She's interrupted you watching 'Harry and Paul', so you quickly pause the programme, minimise the page and give her 'that look' over the top of your glasses, as if to say 'Really? Time off from work of all things?'

Sighing and jogging your right leg back and forth you look at the calendar to see if you can spare her for those few days. The answer is either a begrudging 'yes', or a definite 'no' as the case may be. Either way she leaves your office bearing you malice because of your childish attitude, malice which is soon spread to the other teachers who are of course gathered in the staffroom for their break. You are now officially considered a wanker by the teaching staff.
And if you want to earn their hatred you have the right to cancel leave without notice. The teachers' contracts are a joke. It doesn't matter if they are attending their brother's wedding in Cardiff, or flying to Glasgow to visit an old school friend. Basic humanity doesn't occur to you. Cancel that leave and they will hate you forever!

Here it comes: the all-important Monthly Pay. This generally comes in on time, but is so pitifully small it's nothing worth getting excited over. And it's often wrong! It's never, ever too much, not once have you ever seen a case where someone was overpaid. There is regularly a whole section of the teaching staff who have been underpaid, which leads rise to a reasonably polite British-style clamour. You promise to sort it out. It was your mistake after all! But by now it's too late. Rent, bills, child maintenance, alcohol, the cost of the daily commute all have to be paid for. It's too freaking late. You have finally earned the ever-lasting loathing of your team. Congratulate yourself and treat yourself to another episode of 'Harry and Paul'.

The Students

The students are the reason the school exists, they are the life, blood and soul of the whole creepy set-up. The customer is always right, right? Not here. They are adults, but are treated by the management and admin staff like criminals out on parole.

We've already mentioned the preposterous 'lateness rule' whereby everyone loses out. This is just one in a series of humiliations for a set of mostly hard-working adults trying to do the right thing in their lives. The possibilities here for displaying a breath-taking lack of common decency or humanity are endless in your DOS role.

Bad Attendance

The worst is probably the naughty-step, otherwise known as 'bad attendance'. The people who work at the school, or at least the management, are soundly protected by gutless Employment Laws, which means they can get away with a heck of a lot without being fired. Not so for the poor students, most of whom are on visas, which can be cancelled at any second by the barbarous gang of hooligans known as the UKBA. Any student whose attendance drops below a certain percentage 3 times in a row is out. There are no grounds for mercy, compassion or even simple courtesy and manners.

You, the DOS, are the pitiless enforcer and backer-up of the insane set of 'rules' known as UK Immigration Law. Tears don't work, neither does grovelling (sometimes literally), pleading for mercy, or even the occasional threat of suicide. If the students don't attend classes you report them. And they will hate you for it. You make genuine enemies here, so well done!

The 'Level-up' Farce

During the course of a normal working day there are two reasons why you are perpetually hounded by students during their break. The first is that they don't like their teacher, in which case you do absolutely bugger-all, mostly because it would mean extra admin, a chat with the teacher and all manner of time-wasting. So the student stays with the respective teacher. Eventually either the student or the teacher will leave the school, so problem solved.

The second reason is the thorny issue of students who think they are in the wrong level and want to move up (for example from 'pre-intermediate' to 'intermediate'.) This is a daily headache and is a problem of such volume that it cannot be ignored.

Generally your first move is to tell the student to talk to his teacher. This creates confusion as the teacher told the student to speak to you. More incompetence on your part!

The solution is to put the student down on a list of these budding linguists to take a 'level-up' test on the last Friday of the month. This duly happens, and those that pass will move up to join a course which is generally well underway. These new students will have missed enough of the course to fail the end-of-term exam and so they may as well have stayed put. Those who fail do stay put.

This is all getting a bit technical, so I'll give a pleasant bullet-point list of how to earn your students' dislike, disrespect or even hatred (if you are lucky).

- 'Forget' to put a student's name on the magic list, so when she turns up for the test she's turned away. No arguments. The Golden Rule here is the DOS is always right, not the damn customer.

- Don't inform students they need to bring photo ID to the test, so when they come breezing in armed with nothing but a pen, they are also turned away.
- Enforce the 'lateness rule' again to the point of madness; more students turned away!
- Don't allow reasonable time for the students to finish the test. The final part is always a piece of writing, which when written in a hurry is going to be so full of mistakes you can wave it in their faces as evidence for failure.

The students are far from stupid, they can see what you're doing, so when you humiliate them in the above irrational manner you will have finally earned their hatred too. More congratulations, and as it's Friday treat yourself to a box of Australian Chardonnay! Drink this at home, alone.

Ruining a Perfectly Good Romance

Romantic Relationships

There is a whole raft of self-help books on how to get someone to fall in love you, most of them very creepy indeed as they tend to use certain formulas and methods which could almost be described as 'scientific'. Scientific in the sense that you 'score points' by making yourself appear to be something you are not. I won't go into any more detail here as we'll get bogged down in the 'whys' and the 'wherefores' and we don't particularly care about this process. This is a streamlined book, a thin volume on how to get someone to really hate you. Love doesn't come into it.

Or does it?
For our purposes you are going to have to form a profound romantic relationship with someone, nurture that relationship and then suddenly and clinically behave in a manner that will make your partner really hate your guts forever.

Falling in Love

It doesn't matter how it happens. It could be the fabled 'love at first sight', which in spite of the somewhat obscenely cynical nature of this book, I can claim does actually happen. It could be a colleague or a student (God help you with that one). It could even be a friend you've known for years. Whoever it is, the relationship often follows the same pattern: you want to be in each others' company all the time, you have plenty of sex, you go out and about together, you are known as a couple (unless the relationship is covert). You are all loved up, bless your cotton socks!
This is where you strike, you evil bastard. Your one mission now is to get your partner to hate you. Don't use obvious tactics such as sleeping with other people or just dumping him/her. Where is the fun in that? There are

more subtle techniques, where through playing the long game you can turn your partner right off. We all know the expression 'familiarity breeds contempt'. This is the same concept, except with some interesting additions.

Rapport

By the stage you are sleeping together and are spending a lot of time in each others' company you must have established some kind of strong rapport: a similar sense of humour; a similar cultural background (for example, if you are abroad and come from the same country); you have carefully observed you partner's needs and take care of them. These are examples of the creepy 'point-scoring' I mentioned earlier. These are the conscious aspects. Everything is still peachy, so it's time for you to get to work. You need to start with the subconscious.

We've all noticed that during a conversation with someone we are getting along with we adopt the same position and posture of your interlocutor. If she is leaning forward, you do the same; if he has his hands folded under his chin, then ditto, and so on. If you do this in a way that is not obvious then your rapport will increase. You don't want that at all! You need to do it in a way that is way over the top. Copy every single movement your partner makes to the point where it becomes weird. You've never done this before in your relationship so some degree of confusion should be created. She may think you are messing around, taking the piss and ask you what's up. Deny everything.

The Way she Speaks

As you copy the way she moves, also imitate her speech. If she speaks fast, mimic her tempo; if her voice is quite high-pitched, make yours the same. Everyone has their own way of using their language: accent, vocab, grammar. Listen, study and imitate her to the best of your abilities. By now she's going to think you are not only being weird, but also a childish dickhead. Good! Keep it up. She'll be freaked out and will ask you to stop, but keep it going for the rest of your date. As an added bonus, if you are out having dinner you could 'forget your wallet', so she has to pay for the benefit of experiencing your idiotic behaviour.

Body Language

Everyone is attracted to confident behaviour. Along with confident behaviour comes a certain type of body language. Apparently keeping a straight back is paramount, whether standing or sitting. If you move around with a nice straight back this indicates to the people around you that you are in total possession and control of your actions and are in no way afraid or shy to be in tricky social situations. You exude confidence and this could well be one of the reasons you got together with your partner in the first place. So stay confident, keep a straight back, own the room, until the point when everything in your relationship is just lovely. Then change. Here are a few tips:

- Hunch your back so you are a few inches shorter than you used to be.
- Don't put your hands behind your back.
- Shorten your stride, shuffle along at an irritatingly slow pace, especially in hurried situations such as running for a bus.
- If you drop something on the floor, make it a big deal by becoming embarrassed, red in the face, and looking round furtively to see if anyone else has noticed.
- Keep your hands in your pockets as much as possible. Avoid holding your partner's hand.
- Let yourself go; put on some weight and do no exercise whatsoever.

Again, your partner will be confused by this sudden change in demeanour. She will question you about it, but always deny everything. Eventually this will lead to irritation, some degree of embarrassment on her part, and even anger. These are the seeds of hate.

Other People's Observations

When you got together with your partner there will have been a certain amount of gossip among the people you both know. Similarly, when your behaviour suddenly, and for no apparent reason becomes odd and unattractive, this news will also spread rapidly. This can be vey useful fuel for the fire if you exploit it in the most effective way. The Golden Rule here is that negative news about yourself gets back to your now highly confused loved one.

First, ask one of your friends to meet with your partner in a situation where he can chat about you in an extremely negative light. You've always behaved like this with a girlfriend (it's a pattern); you've started to neglect your personal hygiene again; you've been caught shoplifting; the other day you kicked a springer spaniel puppy on the beach; no, you're not ill or depressed, possibly merely bored with her; but hey! Things could still turn around. He does still say he loves you.

Second, during a date tell your partner you deliberately messed up an important job interview as you didn't want the damn job in the first place. This would make you lose your benefits! Demonstrate a total lack of ambition to get on in life.

Third, talk at length and in juicy detail about your ex-partners, their sexual preferences, how they all dumped you within six months and how you are baffled as to why this happened time and again.

Fourth, and this one cannot be emphasised enough, let your physical appearance go: the greasy hair, the lack of deodorant, the tasty zit on your nose which is just dying to be burst but which you nurture to grotesque proportions, the shoes which are falling to pieces, and so on.

Finally, make it very clear you do not like her friends, want nothing to do with them, and even take the step of asking her to not see them so often. This is a display of irrational and selfish jealously, and believe me, there is no bigger turn off. Linked to this is of course jealousy of her talking to or even looking at other men. Forbid it! And if she defies this unreasonable order, scowl at her from across the room and then interrogate her to within an inch of her life about what she was doing, talking about etc.

Dread and Dislike

By now we are at the start of a tragedy. She loved/loves you and cannot understand your crazy behaviour. Perhaps she dreads meeting you; she certainly dislikes the person you have become. Many of her friends are possibly saying 'get rid, he' s just another dickhead'. But you haven't reached your prized goal of everlasting hatred! You have to keep going and she may think you will change back into the man she fell in love with, so you play your next card. You start messing with her family.

Meeting the Parents

This may sound like an outrageously sweeping statement, but people are very often attracted to someone who resembles one or both of their parents. This is important. Parents loom large in your loved one's life and meeting them for the first time is a very big deal indeed. So here is your big chance. The all-important First Meeting can only happen once!

For this section I'm using the example of a man meeting his female partner's parents. The same general principles apply to any mix of partner genders.

Also worth bearing in mind is the fact that you are being invited to meet them at all. This indicates the relationship is becoming 'serious' in spite of all your clownish antics as detailed earlier. Before the meeting find out which parent your partner prefers (in a lot of cases there will be only one parent so problem solved). Obviously you can't ask 'who do you prefer, your Mum or your Dad'? The main clue is in who she talks about most. Find out as much as you can about their political affiliations, their religious beliefs, what their social status is. Do they (usually the father) support a particular football team? Do they have a pet? Information is indeed power and you can use it to maximum effect during this first meeting. It takes balls, that's for sure, but if used effectively you will find yourself a genuine hate figure.

The Arrival

Ok, so the meeting is set up for a Saturday afternoon at 4pm. There are millions of families up and down the country, of course every single one is different, but when meeting your son or daughter's partner for the first time, afternoon tea would be perhaps the most traditional way to do this.

You need to prepare for this meeting. Make sure you've been out drinking heavily the night before and have had a maximum of three hours sleep; follow this with a few bevvies at lunch-time and you will look suitably flushed and exhausted. You will smell of booze and have bags under your blood-shot eyes. If you are teetotal for whatever reason, then stay up all night playing some kind of hectic computer game. The physical effects of this marathon will appear much the same as a night out on the town. Also, if you are lucky enough to have some benzodiazepines in your possession take a high dose an hour before your arrival so your speech is slurred and you are distinctly unsteady on your feet. So far, so good.

Now, what about your attire? If it's a hot summer's day wear an old T-shirt, Bermuda shorts and flip-flops. The T-shirt should have some kind of dodgy slogan such as 'I love LSD', or 'Fuck the Government'. Something childish, even if you are a man of 40. In the UK the weather is more likely to be chilly, so ripped and dirty jeans and a stained sweatshirt will do nicely. If the family seriously supports a football team then invest in a scarf beforehand. This is easy; just go with their most-hated rivals. If they support Man City, then arrive sporting a Man Utd scarf; if they support Portsmouth, and God help you these days with this, then proudly wear a Southampton one. Millwall versus West Ham is another classic. You get the picture.

So you've arrived at least 45 minutes late. The greeting is one of the most important scenes, as first impressions are formed in less than a minute. Your stumbling and slurring should be obvious but not over the top. Present the mother with some kind of cheap supermarket bouquet of flowers with the price label still attached. The father will want to shake hands. Do not refuse this, but give a very limp handshake. This never goes down well. It denotes timidity, and lack of force and personality. When your handshake is very weak and limp you are perceived as having little love in your nature, no passion or magnetism. Not a great start and you are still in the hallway!

If a dog comes charging through to greet you, make some kind of terrified shriek and stammer that you can't stand dogs, you had a bad experience as a child, you are afraid of being bitten (even if the dog is a totally harmless breed such as a Dachshund or a King Charles Spaniel). Hide behind your girlfriend until the poor beast has been banished from sight. People adore their pets so this is another point in your ever-growing disfavour. This also, along with the limp handshake, demonstrates a distinct lack of 'manliness'.

The parents, expecting a guest, will have made an effort to clean their house in order to impress you with their cleanliness, so be sure to track mud or dust across their pristine carpets or wooden flooring. Do not acknowledge this faux pas. Out of politeness the parents will probably do the same, but it will be noted. By now your girlfriend will be mortified and most likely giving you dirty looks behind her parents' backs. Just smile back at her, give her the thumbs up and shrug your shoulders.

The Drinks

So once you've been ushered through to the living room where the main event is to take place, first sit down in what is clearly the father's arm-chair (never on the sofa, where you will be expected, quite naturally, to sit next to your partner) and stick your feet up on the nearest available piece of furniture. This could be a pouf, another chair, or even the coffee table itself. Blow out through puffed-out cheeks and rake your hand through your hair, which by now should look as though a cow has been chewing on it.

The usual drinks at a British tea-time are tea, coffee, or a soft drink. 'Something stronger' may be offered, but it's unlikely. When asked the inevitable question, 'What can I get you to drink?' you should always answer 'a beer please…have you got any Special Brew?' No they most certainly have not got Special Brew! Go with whatever beer there is. If there's no beer then ask for a vodka and coke. If they don't have even these essential ingredients just accept whatever alcoholic drink there happens to be. Crack some feeble joke about needing a 'hair-of-the-dog'.

The Food

There will be traditional tea-time snacks on offer; cake, biscuits, a bowl of crisps or nuts, possibly some sandwiches. Refuse everything with the words, 'No, I'm alright thanks'. Do not eat a morsel! This is downright rude behavior in any culture; to refuse food which has been prepared specifically for you as the guest of honour. Instead take out a packet of fags and light one up without asking permission. This is a shocking act in 2014 (interestingly, as up to as recently as 1980 it would have been just about OK). You may well be asked to put it out if nobody in the household smokes, in which case you drop it into the dregs of your drink, which you have already finished. If either of the parents does smoke then the simple fact that you neglected to ask permission will act against you.
By now the parents will have formed an impression of you as being ill-mannered, slovenly and possible having some kind of drink problem. Dislike and disappointment will soon turn to hate as you begin to converse.

The Conversation

There are three topics of conversation which must be avoided during conversation with people you don't know, and especially with people you are supposedly trying to impress as their precious daughter's beloved partner. These are politics, religion and money. Why? Because they are thorny issues on which everyone has strong opinions, which are unlikely to change just because of your woolly, badly-thought through, semi-drunken ranting.

Religion

Let's start with the thorniest topic of all; religion. By its very nature religion yields the strongest opinions and emotions because it deals with the Big Questions: Is there a God, and if so, what kind? Is there an after-life? It affects your actions throughout your entire life. It's very often associated with your upbringing and your parents' beliefs. It concerns belonging to a certain community of people who all share the same belief system. It underpins your morals and ethical stance. Your religious community's views of people who do not share the same belief system can be virulent and irrational. There is often no room for manoeuvre. You know what I'm talking about. Avoid this topic at all costs!

Except of course, you don't. You want your girlfriend's (although by this stage, as you sit there completely at your ease sipping your 3rd drink, she could well have become in her own mind your ex-girlfriend) parents to hate you. So you start denigrating their religion as far and as fast as possible. For this purpose, I'm going to use Roman Catholicism and Atheism as the two protagonist arguments. These are purely random. I could have used Mormonism, Buddhism, Islam, Hinduism, Shamanism or Satanism; whatever, the outcome is going to be the same.

As your partner's family are Roman Catholics there is likely to be an image of Mary Mother of God somewhere in the living room. Point at it and ask who it is; a relative perhaps, or a painting by a local artist. This breath-taking display of ignorance will hopefully shock them into a brief description of their religious beliefs. You reply that you are an Atheist, you don't believe in any giant bearded weirdo floating on a cloud. Explain in minute detail Richard Dawkins' 'Teapot Theory'. This can be found in his book 'The God Delusion' and is bound to offend your audience as it is hard to refute. So let's move on, enough damage has been done with religion.

Politics

This is a much easier one to deal with than religion. In spite of your seemingly blasé attitude you've actually been working hard to earn everyone's disrespect. Ask for another drink and then enquire as to which party they voted for at the last general election. You can see the way this is going, can't you? (Another quick disclaimer, I am not intending to denigrate or affiliate myself, the author, with any political point of view). Let's say they voted Labour. At this point you roll your eyes and mutter some kind of just-about inaudible expletive. If they voted Labour, you voted UKIP. Bring up their immigration policies, support the UK's exit from the European Union, praise Nigel Farage to the skies. On no account provide any convincing or cogent argument to back up your slurred and slumped opinions. Finish with your whole-hearted agreement with UKIP Councillor David Silvester's view that the unprecedented flooding of early 2014 was caused by the Marriage (Same Sex Couples) Act.

With this last bombshell your girlfriend's parents will not only heartily dislike you as a person, they may already actually hate you! And who can blame them? You've been acting like a total arse from the moment of your arrival. God only knows what your partner is thinking.

Money

Leave the subject of money as the last one, as it's the easiest to deal with. You need to be at least level-headed enough to mess things up even more, and by now you are fairly well pole-axed on whatever alcoholic drink they are so kind as to be topping you up with and you've been snorting speed during your numerous 'bathroom breaks' (be sure to splash urine liberally around the toilet seat and on the bath mat). Ask what jobs they have and how much they earn. Enquire as to whether any of the furniture or their car is on finance and if they manage to keep up with the payments. Tell them you could get a good deal for them on whatever objects happen to be adorning the room. You could even sell their dog to some travellers you know to use for hare coursing (although if it's a Dachshund that might be stretching it a little, but what the hell…).

Complete your inebriated tirade and interrogation with a mostly incoherent explanation of why you have no intention of actually getting a job as you can live quite nicely off benefits and selling 'a bit of weed'.

Outstay your welcome. By the time they finally ask you to leave I guarantee they will loathe, detest and hate you. They will doubt your sanity and be appalled by your lack of sobriety. Your girlfriend will now assuredly be your ex-girlfriend. If you are lucky she'll follow you out onto the street and dump you there and then. Yet more congratulations are in order! Treat yourself to an all-night amphetamine session. Alone.

Part 4: The Impossible Dream

Can you be Hated by Everyone?

The answer to this question is unfortunately a resounding 'No'. Even the most extreme cases of those rare people who can be described as evil have their supporters. Hitler has his neo-Nazis; a surprisingly large number of Russians still remember and support Stalin. I think you'll agree, though, that Hitler and Stalin, in theory and practice, have earned the hatred of their fellow humans.

But as I pointed out at the start of this short book, we are concerned with the everyday, petty kind of hatred you find on buses, in shops, in cinemas and at petrol stations. We want to make that leap from mere 'existension' to loathing. The scope here for you to be hated is endless, so the final part of this book is to be dedicated to your local community.

We've already been through quite a few case studies, you've been reading this book for an hour or so, you get the picture, therefore I'll keep this section brief.
So then, who can we mess with on a daily basis?

The Postman

The traditional enemy of the postman is the dog. There are many confrontations up and down the country every day, usually leading to the postman being bitten. If you have this kind of savage beast in your domestic set-up, do not use it! A dog is not a weapon! There is a real danger of the postman hating the dog and not you. You must replace the canine's rather crude defensive tactic with some particularly irritating mind games. So, here's a list of possible methods you can use to earn the hatred of your long-suffering postman:

- When you first move in to your new home, accost the postman every time you see him, whether he has something for you or not. Detain him with friendly and inane chit-chat. If he has no post for you ask him if he's sure and try to look in his bag. This will annoy him. Keep this up day after day, week after week.

- Startle him by suddenly and violently opening your front door just as he's about to post something through your letterbox. Make this as dramatic as possible. He will now think you are mad as well as annoying. But what about that final step to hatred?

- Whenever he asks you to sign for something, refuse to do so. Just don't do it; accuse him of trying to defraud you of something (although don't specify as to what this might be). When he's gone call his manager and make a formal complaint, which these days will have to be looked into, even if sounds utterly outrageous or untrue. Your postman will now hate you; I guarantee it.

The Newsagent

This poor guy, the newsagent (I'm assuming it's a guy for the sake of convenience, not because of any sexist issue, subconscious or otherwise), has a tough job. It appears easy enough, standing there behind his counter selling all manner of expensive produce (most of which you could buy at the supermarket if you could be arsed to go there), chatting to customers if he's not one of those strangely surly types. He's there from very early in the morning until late at night, possibly seven days a week. A tough job. There are certain aspects of this job that all newsagents hate, so in order to earn that hate you should exploit them to the max:

- Animals in his shop. It's easy to understand why he doesn't want an animal in his shop. They can make a mess, they can scare the other customers, and these days there are all kinds of allergies to take into account. So go in on a daily basis with some kind of large beast. Maybe a big dog, a Rottweiler or a St Bernard; make sure the animal is off the lead to maximise its potential for scaring other customers. The newsagent will ask you to tie the dog up outside. Always come out with some uesless answer such as, 'sorry mate, don't have a lead', or, 'don't worry, he's harmless'. Even better would be an alpaca! Stand there scratching your head as you scrutinise the tinned soup, apparently oblivious to the fact that your alpaca is munching away in the fruit and vegetable section.
  You now have the newsagent's attention; he knows who you are and he doesn't like you.

- Newsagents don't like having lots of school kids in their shop. They too make a mess; they can put off other customers by forming a huge queue at the check out; they indulge in shoplifting. If you are a TEFL teacher here is a golden opportunity. Tell your class of 30 Euro kids that as part of their learning programme they will be practising their English in a real live shop! Take them all in at once; it will be chaos. When they are actually paying for their goods make sure they say everything in correct English and if they don't, ask them to repeat it. This will really mess up the newsagent's day if you go in several times with different classes. If he doesn't hate you by now then he certainly will after the next easy-to-use tip.

- By nine or ten o'clock in the evening the newsagent is ready to close. He's knackered; he has to be back there in six hours to sort out the damn newspapers. He wants to get some sleep. So if he closes at nine, go into the shop at exactly one minute before absolutely smashed on strong lager (possibly with your alpaca in tow). Wander around without a basket picking up random items: tins of beans, tampons, ice cream, a bottle of red wine. These items will soon stack up in your arms so you'll start to drop them. Make sure one of these is a bottle of red wine, which will of course smash everywhere. The newsagent will be hating your guts by this stage. Ask more idiotic questions such as, 'where are your chicken tikkas boss?' or 'do you sell those little plastic forks'? After around ten minutes of this appalling behaviour the newsagent will have to say something to get rid of you. Whatever it is he says, no matter how polite, take great drunken offense, dump your items on the counter and storm out. Do this two or three times a week.

Summing up

So we can see how easy it is to earn the hatred of the people who make up your local community. I could continue, but I think we've had enough now.

I could detail how to get yourself banned from your local library, or how to profoundly upset the ice cream van woman. I could even tell you how to really piss off a policemen, simply by relentlessly asking a series of vacuous questions such as:

- Where's the nearest health spa?
- What kind of fishing rod would you recommend for fishing off the pier?
- What should I do if my alpaca gets stuck up a tree?
- (Standing outside a pub) Where's the nearest pub?
- How many times have you used your piece in the course of duty?

Hatred is exhausting. As I pointed out at the start of the book the word 'hate' is a strong one. Every time we hear this word it's like a small blow from an ice pick to the forehead. This book may raise eyebrows, it may ruffle feathers, but so what? I think the spirit of what I am trying to get across is summed up nicely by the following image:

31

Made in the USA
Middletown, DE
22 March 2022

63052720R00020